I love Dad

Doting Dads love
their children—no matter
what species they are.

We all need our Dads
to protect, support,
and care for us.

Baby animals listen to
their Dads and learn
from them every day,
just like we do.

I have some friends over for a playdate. Dad's in charge, so we are going to play some ice-cool games.

Life on the frozen Antarctic is hard, so it takes a whole community of emperor penguins to rear chicks. Dads do more than their fair share. They look after the eggs, and they also take care of groups of chicks when Mom goes fishing.

My **Dad** is the **best.** He lets me **sleep** on his **back** for hours and **he never complains.**

Big daddy mountain gorillas are called silverbacks. They are gentle with young gorillas and happily play with them, but they will fight to the death if they have to protect their families.

Hooray, I made it out alive! Time to hop off...

Darwin's frogs make devoted dads. Tadpoles grow inside a special pouch in their father's throat, where they are safe from predators. He gives birth by spitting them out when they have grown into little froglets.

You cover me with love, Dad, and I know you will keep me safe.

Meerkats live in large groups made up of three families. Dads are in charge of keeping a lookout for dangerous animals. They bark loudly if they are worried for the youngsters' safety and everyone flees underground.

Hey Dad, Mom's not watching— so let's go faster!

Male swans are called cobs, and they are very protective of their families. Young swans are called cygnets, and Dad often takes them for rides on his back.

The world can seem like a scary place. That's why we stay close to Dad.

Sea horses are strange-looking, slow-swimming fish. A father keeps up to 2,000 eggs in his pouch while they grow. He gives birth to his tiny babies after just two to four weeks.

Thanks for making the world a rosy place. Pink is my favorite color!

Flamingo parents help each other to build a mud nest and take care of their chick. These big water birds have pink feathers because they eat pink food!

Look how big I am, Dad. I'm even taller than you now!

Monkeys live in families, and just like human families, they come in all types and sizes. Most macaque families are large. They squabble, cuddle, and care for each other.

How can I fall asleep when you snore SO loudly, Dad?

Male lions are sleepy animals, but they still find time to look after the cubs when lionesses go hunting.

I know **Dad** is always right. I heard it straight from the **horse's mouth!**

Mustangs are a type of horse that live wild and free in American grasslands. A male mustang is called a stallion, and he guards his family from danger.

Dad says he loves us all the same, so why does he keep forgetting our names?

Male jawfish hide inside a sandy burrow on the sea floor. Fish eggs are a tasty treat for many sea-living creatures, so these crafty Dads keep their eggs safe in their mouths while they grow. When the eggs hatch, the tiny fish will swim away from Dad.

My Dad has the best mustache in the world. I am trying to grow one just like him.

A male emperor tamarin acts as a midwife, helping his partner to give birth to their young. He then carries the babies on his back, bringing them back to Mom when it is time for her to feed them milk.

Hey **Dad,** tell me how things were **back** in your day. I **love** to hear your **tales.**

A warthog family is called a sounder. Although males don't normally stay with a sounder, they do stay nearby and come to visit the family. They have four large tusks that are used for digging and fighting.

Dad,
you know
everything.
How did you get
so wise?

Great horned owls are huge,
powerful hunters of the night sky.
Mom and Dad hoot to each other,
and they share the care of their
fluffy chicks until they are old
enough to fly away.

Here are three ways to show Dad you love him.

Laugh at his jokes!

♥

Give him a big hug.

♥

Thank him for looking after you.

Can you think of any more?

Editor: Tasha Percy
Editorial Assistant: Joanna McInerney
Editorial Director: Victoria Garrard
Designer: Natalie Godwin
Art Director: Laura Roberts-Jensen
Publisher: Zeta Jones

Photo credits
(t=top, b=bottom, l=left, r=right, c=center, fc=front cover)
1c: Visuals Unlimited: Reinhard Dirscher, 2l: Biosphoto: Patrick Kinetz-D, 3r: Shutterstock: Background, 4l: Shutterstock: Background, 5r: Getty Images: Mint Imags-Franss Lanting, 6l: Getty Images: Art Wolfe, 7r: istockphoto.com: Background, 8l: istockphoto.com: Background, , 9r: Getty Images: Michael and Patricia Fogden/Mind, 10l: Getty Images: Paul Souders, 11r: istockphoto.com: Background, 12l: Shutterstock: Background, 13r: Getty Images: Straublund Photography, 14l: Monterey Bay Aquarium: Randy Wilder, 15r: istockphoto.com: Background, 16l: istockphoto.com: Background, 17r NaturePL: Dave Watts, 18l: NaturePL: Delpho/ARCO, 19r: istockphoto.com: Background, 20l; Shutterstock: Background, 21r: Getty Images: Paul Mansfield, 22l: NaturePL: Carol Walker, 23r: Shutterstock: Background, 24l: Shutterstock: Background, 25r: Oceanwide Images: Yellowhead Jawfish 45M1030-10, 26l: NautrePL: Mark Bowler, 27r: istockphoto.com: Background, 28l: istockphoto.com: Background, 29r: Getty Images: Richard Du Toit/Minden Pictures: 30l: Getty Images: Daniel Cox, 31r: istockphoto.com: Background, 32c: Shutterstock: Background